The Gateless Gate

By

Ekai, called Mu-mon

Translated by

Nyogen Senzaki and Paul Reps

First published in 1934

Published by Left of Brain Books

Copyright © 2023 Left of Brain Books

ISBN 978-1-397-66862-2

First Edition

All rights reserved. No part of this publication may be reproduced, distributed, or transmitted in any form or by any means, including photocopying, recording, or other electronic or mechanical methods, without the prior written permission of the publisher, except in the case of brief quotations permitted by copyright law. Left of Brain Books is a division of Left Of Brain Onboarding Pty Ltd.

PUBLISHER'S PREFACE

About the Book

"Koans are a Zen Buddhist spiritual technique which use word-play to achieve enlightenment. They frequently involve absurd or contradictory statements, which are intended to create extreme cognitive dissonance in the mind of the pupil. As such, their actual content or structure is not as important as the mental state which they induce. This collection includes some of the most famous koans, such as Tozan's "three pounds of flax":

What is the Buddha? -- This flax weighs three pounds.

and Baso's conundrum:
What is Buddha? -- This mind is not Buddha.

as well as some involving bizarre behavior, such as Nansen Cuts the Cat in Two and Blow out the Candle.

While short and succinct, this book has enormous depth, and offers new rewards on repeated readings."

(Quote from sacred-texts.com)

CONTENTS

PUBLISHER'S PREFACE
- JOSHU'S DOG 1
- HYAKUJO'S FOX 3
- GUTEI'S FINGER 6
- A BEARDLESS FOREIGNER 7
- KYOGEN MOUNTS THE TREE 8
- BUDDHA TWIRLS A FLOWER 9
- JOSHU WASHES THE BOWL 10
- KEICHU'S WHEEL 11
- A BUDDHA BEFORE HISTORY 12
- SEIZEI ALONE AND POOR 13
- JOSHU EXAMINES A MONK IN MEDITATION 14
- ZUIGAN CALLS HIS OWN MASTER 16
- TOKUSAN HOLDS HIS BOWL 17
- NANSEN CUTS THE CAT IN TWO 18
- TOZAN'S THREE BLOWS 19
- BELLS AND ROBES 21
- THE THREE CALLS OF THE EMPEROR'S TEACHER 22
- TOZAN'S THREE POUNDS 24
- EVERYDAY LIFE IS THE PATH 25
- THE ENLIGHTENED MAN 26
- DRIED DUNG 27
- KASHAPA'S PREACHING SIGN 28
- DO NOT THINK GOOD, DO NOT THINK NOT-GOOD .. 29
- WITHOUT WORDS, WITHOUT SILENCE 31
- PREACHING FROM THE THIRD SEAT 32
- TWO MONKS ROLL UP THE SCREEN 33
- IT IS NOT MIND, IT IS NOT BUDDHA, IT IS NOT THINGS 34
- BLOW OUT THE CANDLE 35
- NOT THE WIND, NOT THE FLAG 37
- THIS MIND IS BUDDHA 38
- JOSHU INVESTIGATES 39
- A PHILOSOPHER ASKS BUDDHA 40

- THIS MIND IS NOT BUDDHA 41
- LEARNING IS NOT THE PATH 42
- TWO SOULS 43
- MEETING A ZEN MASTER ON THE ROAD 44
- A BUFFALO PASSES THROUGH THE ENCLOSURE 45
- AN OAK TREE IN THE GARDEN 46
- UMMON'S SIDETRACK 47
- TIPPING OVER A WATER VASE 48
- BODHIDHARMA PACIFIES THE MIND 49
- THE GIRL COMES OUT FROM MEDITATION 50
- SHUZAN'S SHORT STAFF 52
- BASHO'S STAFF 53
- WHO IS HE? 54
- PROCEED FROM THE TOP OF THE POLE 55
- THREE GATES OF TOSOTSU 56
- ONE ROAD OF KEMBO 57
- AMBAN'S ADDITION 58

JOSHU'S DOG

A monk asked Joshu, a Chinese Zen master: "Has a dog Buddha-nature or not?"

Joshu answered: "Mu." [Mu is the negative symbol in Chinese, meaning "No thing" or "Nay."]

Mumon's comment: To realize Zen one has to pass through the barrier of the patriarchs. Enlightenment always comes after the road of thinking is blocked. If you do not pass the barrier of the patriarchs or if your thinking road is not blocked, whatever you think, whatever you do, is like a tangling ghost. You may ask: What is a barrier of a patriarch? This one word, Mu, is it.

This is the barrier of Zen. If you pass through it you will see Joshu face to face. Then you can work hand in hand with the whole line of patriarchs. Is this not a pleasant thing to do?

If you want to pass this barrier, you must work through every bone in your body, through every pore of your skin, filled with this question: What is Mu? and carry it day and night. Do not believe it is the common negative symbol meaning nothing. It is not nothingness, the opposite of existence. If you really want to pass this barrier, you should feel like drinking a hot iron ball that you can neither swallow nor spit out.

Then your previous lesser knowledge disappears. As a fruit ripening in season, your subjectivity and objectivity naturally become one. It is like a dumb man who has had a dream. He knows about it but he cannot tell it.

When he enters this condition his ego-shell is crushed and he can shake the heaven and move the earth. He is like a great warrior with a sharp sword. If a Buddha stands in his way, he will cut him down; if a patriarch offers him any obstacle, he will kill him; and he will be free in his way of birth and death. He can enter any world as if it were his own playground. I will tell you how to do this with this koan:

Just concentrate your whole energy into this Mu, and do not allow any discontinuation. When you enter this Mu and there is no discontinuation, your attainment will be as a candle burning and illuminating the whole universe.

> Has a dog Buddha-nature?
> This is the most serious question of all.
> If you say yes or no,
> You lose your own Buddha-nature.

HYAKUJO'S FOX

Once when Hyakujo delivered some Zen lectures an old man attended them, unseen by the monks. At the end of each talk when the monks left so did he. But one day he remained after they had gone, and Hyakujo asked him: "Who are you?"

The old man replied: "I am not a human being, but I was a human being when the Kashapa Buddha preached in this world. I was a Zen master and lived on this mountain. At that time one of my students asked me whether or not the enlightened man is subject to the law of causation. I answered him: 'The enlightened man is not subject to the law of causation.' For this answer evidencing a clinging to absoluteness I became a fox for five hundred rebirths, and I am still a fox. Will you save me from this condition with your Zen words and let me get out of a fox's body? Now may I ask you: Is the enlightened man subject to the law of causation?"

Hyakujo said: "The enlightened man is one with the law of causation."

At the words of Hyakujo the old man was enlightened. "I am emancipated," he said, paying homage with a deep bow. "I am no more a fox, but I have to leave my body in my dwelling place behind this mountain. Please perform my funeral as a monk." Then he disappeared.

The next day Hyakujo gave an order through the chief monk to prepare to attend the funeral of a monk. "No one was sick in the infirmary," wondered the monks. "What does our teacher mean?"

After dinner Hyakujo led the monks out and around the mountain. In a cave, with his staff he poked out the corpse of an old fox and then performed the ceremony of cremation.

That evening Hyakujo gave a talk to the monks and told them this story about the law of causation.

Obaku, upon hearing the story, asked Hyakujo: "I understand that a long time ago because a certain person gave a wrong Zen answer he became a fox for five hundred rebirths. Now I want to ask: If some modern master is asked many questions and he always gives the right answer, what will become of him?"

Hyakujo said: "You come here near me and I will tell you."

Obaku went near Hyakujo and slapped the teacher's face with his hand, for he knew this was the answer his teacher intended to give him.

Hyakujo clapped his hands and laughed at this discernment. "I thought a Persian had a red beard," he said, "and now I know a Persian who has a red beard."

Mumon's comment: "The enlightened man is not subject." How can this answer make the monk a fox?

"The enlightened man is one with the law of causation." How can this answer make the fox emancipated?

To understand this clearly one has to have just one eye.

        Controlled or not controlled?

The same dice shows two faces.
Not controlled or controlled,
Both are a grievous error.

GUTEI'S FINGER

Gutei raised his finger whenever he was asked a question about Zen. A boy attendant began to imitate him in this way. When anyone asked the boy what his master had preached about, the boy would raise his finger.

Gutei heard about the boy's mischief. He seized him and cut off his finger. The boy cried and ran away. Gutei called and stopped him. When the boy turned his head to Gutei, Gutei raised up his own finger. In that instant the boy was enlightened.

When Gutei was about to pass from this world he gathered his monks around him. "I attained my finger-Zen," he said, "from my teacher Tenryu, and in my whole life I could not exhaust it." Then he passed away.

Mumon's comment: Enlightenment, which Gutei and the boy attained, has nothing to do with a finger. If anyone clings to a finger, Tenryu will be so disappointed that he will annihilate Gutei, the boy, and the clinger all together.

> Gutei cheapens the teaching of Tenryu,
> Emancipating the boy with a knife.
> Compared to the Chinese god who pushed aside a mountain with one hand
> Old Gutei is a poor imitator.

A BEARDLESS FOREIGNER

Wakuan complained when he saw a picture of bearded Bodhidharma: "Why hasn't that fellow a beard?"

Mumon's comment: If you want to study Zen, you must study it with your heart. When you attain realization, it must be true realization. You yourself must have the face of the great Bodhidharma to see him. Just one such glimpse will be enough. But if you say you met him, you never saw him at all.

> One should not discuss a dream
> In front of a simpleton.
> Why has Bodhidharma no beard?
> What an absurd question!

KYOGEN MOUNTS THE TREE

Kyogen said: "Zen is like a man hanging in a tree by his teeth over a precipice. His hands grasp no branch, his feet rest on no limb, and under the tree another person asks him: 'Why did Bodhidharma come to China from India?'

"If the man in the tree does not answer, he fails; and if he does answer, he falls and loses his life. Now what shall he do?"

Mumon's comment: In such a predicament the most talented eloquence is of no use. If you have memorized all the sutras, you cannot use them. When you can give the right answer, even though your past road was one of death, you open up a new road of life. But if you cannot answer, you should live ages hence and ask the future Buddha, Maitreya.

> Kyogen is truly a fool
> Spreading that ego-killing poison
> That closes his pupils' mouths
> And lets their tears stream from their dead eyes.

BUDDHA TWIRLS A FLOWER

When Buddha was in Grdhrakuta mountain he turned a flower in his fingers and held it before his listeners. Every one was silent. Only Maha-Kashapa smiled at this revelation, although he tried to control the lines of his face.

Buddha said: "I have the eye of the true teaching, the heart of Nirvana, the true aspect of non-form, and the ineffable stride of Dharma. It is not expressed by words, but especially transmitted beyond teaching. This teaching I have given to Maha-Kashapa."

Mumon's comment: Golden-faced Gautama thought he could cheat anyone. He made the good listeners as bad, and sold dog meat under the sign of mutton. And he himself thought it was wonderful. What if all the audience had laughed together? How could he have transmitted the teaching? And again, if Maha-Kashapa had not smiled, how could he have transmitted the teaching? If he says that realization can be transmitted, he is like the city slicker that cheats the country dub, and if he says it cannot be transmitted, why does he approve of Maha-Kashapa?

> At the turning of a flower
> His disguise was exposed.
> No one in heaven or earth can surpass
> Maha-Kashapa's wrinkled face.

JOSHU WASHES THE BOWL

A monk told Joshu: "I have just entered the monastery. Please teach me."

Joshu asked: "Have you eaten your rice porridge?"

The monk replied: "I have eaten."

Joshu said: "Then you had better wash your bowl."

At that moment the monk was enlightened.

Mumon's comment: Joshu is the man who opens his mouth and shows his heart. I doubt if this monk really saw Joshu's heart. I hope he did not mistake the bell for a pitcher.

> It is too clear and so it is hard to see.
> A dunce once searched for a fire with a lighted lantern.
> Had he known what fire was,
> He could have cooked his rice much sooner.

KEICHU'S WHEEL

Getsuan said to his students: "Keichu, the first wheel-maker of China, made two wheels of fifty spokes each. Now, suppose you removed the nave uniting the spokes. What would become of the wheel? And had Keichu done this, could he be called the master wheel-maker?"

Mumon's comment: If anyone can answer this question instantly, his eyes will be like a comet and his mind like a flash of lightning.

> When the hubless wheel turns,
> Master or no master can stop it.
> It turns above heaven and below earth,
> South, north, east, and west.

A BUDDHA BEFORE HISTORY

A monk asked Seijo: "I understand that a Buddha who lived before recorded history sat in meditation for ten cycles of existence and could not realize the highest truth, and so could not become fully emancipated. Why was this so?"

Seijo replied: "Your question is self-explanatory."

The monk asked: "Since the Buddha was meditating, why could he not fulfill Buddhahood?"

Seijo said: "He was not a Buddha."

Mumon's comment: I will allow his realization, but I will not admit his understanding. When one ignorant attains realization he is a saint. When a saint begins to understand he is ignorant.

> It is better to realize mind than body.
> When mind is realized one need not worry about body.
> When mind and body become one
> The man is free. Then he desires no praising.

SEIZEI ALONE AND POOR

A monk named Seizei asked of Sozan: "Seizei is alone and poor. Will you give him support?"

Sozan asked: "Seizei?"

Seizei responded: "Yes, sir."

Sozan said: "You have Zen, the best wine in China, and already have finished three cups, and still you are saying that they did not even wet your lips."

Mumon's comment: Seizei overplayed his hand. Why was it so? Because Sozan had eyes and knew with whom to deal. Even so, I want to ask: At what point did Seizei drink wine?

> The poorest man in China,
> The bravest man in China,
> He barely sustains himself,
> Yet wishes to rival the wealthiest.

JOSHU EXAMINES A MONK IN MEDITATION

Joshu went to a place where a monk had retired to meditate and asked him: "What is, is what?"

The monk raised his fist.

Joshu replied: "Ships cannot remain where the water is too shallow." And he left.

A few days later Joshu went again to visit the monk and asked the same question.

The monk answered the same way.

Joshu said: "Well given, well taken, well killed, well saved." And he bowed to the monk.

Mumon's comment: The raised fist was the same both times. Why is it Joshu did not admit the first and approved the second one? Where is the fault?

Whoever answers this knows that Joshu's tongue has no bone so he can use it freely. Yet perhaps Joshu is wrong. Or, through that monk, he may have discovered his mistake.

If anyone thinks that the one's insight exceeds the other's, he has no eyes.

> The light of the eyes is as a comet,
> And Zen's activity is as lightning.

The sword that kills the man
Is the sword that saves the man.

ZUIGAN CALLS HIS OWN MASTER

Zuigan called out to himself every day: "Master."

Then he answered himself: "Yes, sir."

And after that he added: "Become sober."

Again he answered: "Yes, sir."

"And after that," he continued, "do not be deceived by others."

"Yes, sir; yes, sir," he answered.

Mumon's comment: Old Zuigan sells out and buys himself. He is opening a puppet show. He uses one mask to call "Master" and another that answers the master. Another mask says "Sober up" and another, "Do not be cheated by others." If anyone clings to any of his masks, he is mistaken, yet if he imitates Zuigan, he will make himself fox-like.

Some Zen students do not realize the true man in a mask
Because they recognize ego-soul.
Ego-soul is the seed of birth and death,
And foolish people call it the true man.

TOKUSAN HOLDS HIS BOWL

Tokusan went to the dining room from the meditation hall holding his bowl. Seppo was on duty cooking. When he met Tokusan he said: "The dinner drum is not yet beaten. Where are you going with your bowl?"

So Tokusan returned to his room.

Seppo told Ganto about this. Ganto said: "Old Tokusan did not understand ultimate truth."

Tokusan heard of this remark and asked Ganto to come to him. "I have heard," he said, "you are not approving my Zen." Ganto admitted this indirectly. Tokusan said nothing.

The next day Tokusan delivered an entirely different kind of lecture to the monks. Ganto laughed and clapped his hands, saying: "I see our old man understands ultimate truth indeed. None in China can surpass him."

Mumon's comment: Speaking about ultimate truth, both Ganto and Tokusan did not even dream it. After all, they are dummies.

> Whoever understands the first truth
> Should understand the ultimate truth.
> The last and first,
> Are they not the same?

NANSEN CUTS THE CAT IN TWO

Nansen saw the monks of the eastern and western halls fighting over a cat. He seized the cat and told the monks: "If any of you say a good word, you can save the cat."

No one answered. So Nansen boldly cut the cat in two pieces.

That evening Joshu returned and Nansen told him about this. Joshu removed his sandals and, placing them on his head, walked out.

Nansen said: "If you had been there, you could have saved the cat."

Mumon's comment: Why did Joshu put his sandals on his head? If anyone answers this question, he will understand exactly how Nansen enforced the edict. If not, he should watch his own head.

>
> Had Joshu been there,
> He would have enforced the edict oppositely.
> Joshu snatches the sword
> And Nansen begs for his life.

TOZAN'S THREE BLOWS

Tozan went to Ummon. Ummon asked him where he had come from.

Tozan said: "From Sato village."

Ummon asked: "In what temple did you remain for the summer?"

Tozan replied: "The temple of Hoji, south of the lake."

"When did you leave there?" asked Ummon, wondering how long Tozan would continue with such factual answers.

"The twenty-fifth of August," answered Tozan.

Ummon said: "I should give you three blows with a stick, but today I forgive you."

The next day Tozan bowed to Ummon and asked: "Yesterday you forgave me three blows. I do not know why you thought me wrong."

Ummon, rebuking Tozan's spiritless responses, said: "You are good for nothing. You simply wander from one monastery to another."

Before Ummon's words were ended Tozan was enlightened.

Mumon's comment: Ummon fed Tozan good Zen food. If Tozan can digest it, Ummon may add another member to his family.

In the evening Tozan swam around in a sea of good and bad, but at dawn Ummon crushed his nut shell. After all, he wasn't so smart.

Now, I want to ask: Did Tozan deserve the three blows? If you say yes, not only Tozan but every one of you deserves them. If you say no, Ummon is speaking a lie. If you answer this question clearly, you can eat the same food as Tozan.

> The lioness teaches her cubs roughly;
> The cubs jump and she knocks them down.
> When Ummon saw Tozan his first arrow was light;
> His second arrow shot deep.

BELLS AND ROBES

Ummon asked: "The world is such a wide world, why do you answer a bell and don ceremonial robes?"

Mumon's comment: When one studies Zen one need not follow sound or color or form. Even though some have attained insight when hearing a voice or seeing a color or a form, this is a very common way. It is not true Zen. The real Zen student controls sound, color, form, and actualizes the truth in his everyday life.

Sound comes to the ear, the ear goes to sound. When you blot out sound and sense, what do you understand? While listening with ears one never can understand. To understand intimately one should see sound.

> When you understand, you belong to the family;
> When you do not understand, you are a stranger.
> Those who do not understand belong to the family,
> And when they understand they are strangers.

THE THREE CALLS OF THE EMPEROR'S TEACHER

Chu, called Kokushi, the teacher of the emperor, called to his attendant: "Oshin."

Oshin answered: "Yes."

Chu repeated, to test his pupil: "Oshin."

Oshin repeated: "Yes."

Chu called: "Oshin."

Oshin answered: "Yes."

Chu said: "I ought to apologize to you for all this calling, but really you ought to apologize to me."

Mumon's comment: When old Chu called Oshin three times his tongue was rotting, but when Oshin answered three times his words were brilliant. Chu was getting decrepit and lonesome, and his method of teaching was like holding a cow's head to feed it clover.

Oshin did not trouble to show his Zen either. His satisfied stomach had no desire to feast. When the country is prosperous everyone is indolent; when the home is wealthy the children are spoiled.

Now I want to ask you: Which one should apologize?

When prison stocks are iron and have no place for the head, the prisoner is doubly in trouble.
When there is no place for Zen in the head of our generation, it is in grievous trouble.
If you try to hold up the gate and door of a falling house,
You also will be in trouble.

TOZAN'S THREE POUNDS

A monk asked Tozan when he was weighing some flax: "What is Buddha?"

Tozan said: "This flax weighs three pounds."

Mumon's comment: Old Tozan's Zen is like a clam. The minute the shell opens you see the whole inside. However, I want to ask you: Do you see the real Tozan?

> Three pounds of flax in front of your nose,
> Close enough, and mind is still closer.
> Whoever talks about affirmation and negation
> Lives in the right and wrong region.

EVERYDAY LIFE IS THE PATH

Joshu asked Nansen: "What is the path?"

Nansen said: "Everyday life is the path."

Joshu asked: "Can it be studied?"

Nansen said: "If you try to study, you will be far away from it."

Joshu asked: "If I do not study, how can I know it is the path?"

Nansen said: "The path does not belong to the perception world, neither does it belong to the nonperception world. Cognition is a delusion and noncognition is senseless. If you want to reach the true path beyond doubt, place yourself in the same freedom as sky. You name it neither good nor not-good."

At these words Joshu was enlightened.

Mumon's comment: Nansen could melt Joshu's frozen doubts at once when Joshu asked his questions. I doubt though if Joshu reached the point that Nansen did. He needed thirty more years of study.

In spring, hundreds of flowers; in autumn, a harvest moon;
In summer, a refreshing breeze; in winter, snow will accompany you.
If useless things do not hang in your mind,
Any season is a good season for you.

THE ENLIGHTENED MAN

Shogen asked: "Why does the enlightened man not stand on his feet and explain himself?" And he also said: "It is not necessary for speech to come from the tongue."

Mumon's comment: Shogen spoke plainly enough, but how many will understand? If anyone comprehends, he should come to my place and test out my big stick. Why, look here, to test real gold you must see it through fire.

If the feet of enlightenment moved, the great ocean would overflow;
If that head bowed, it would look down upon the heavens.
Such a body has no place to rest. . . .
Let another continue this poem.

DRIED DUNG

A monk asked Ummon: "What is Buddha?"

Ummon answered him: "Dried dung."

Mumon's comment: It seems to me Ummon is so poor he cannot distinguish the taste of one food from another, or else he is too busy to write readable letters. Well, he tried to hold his school with dried dung. And his teaching was just as useless.

> Lightning flashes,
> Sparks shower.
> In one blink of your eyes
> You have missed seeing.

KASHAPA'S PREACHING SIGN

Ananda asked Kashapa: "Buddha gave you the golden-woven robe of successorship. What else did he give you?"

Kashapa said: "Ananda."

Ananda answered: "Yes, brother."

Said Kashapa: "Now you can take down my preaching sign and put up your own."

Mumon's comment: If one understands this, he will see the old brotherhood still gathering, but if not, even though he has studied the truth from ages before the Buddhas, he will not attain enlightenment.

The point of the question is dull but the answer is intimate.
How many persons hearing it will open their eyes?
Elder brother calls and younger brother answers,
This spring does not belong to the ordinary season.

DO NOT THINK GOOD, DO NOT THINK NOT-GOOD

When he became emancipated the sixth patriarch received from the fifth patriarch the bowl and robe given from the Buddha to his successors, generation after generation.

A monk named E-myo out of envy pursued the patriarch to take this great treasure away from him. The sixth patriarch placed the bowl and robe on a stone in the road and told E-myo: "These objects just symbolize the faith. There is no use fighting over them. If you desire to take them, take them now."

When E-myo went to move the bowl and robe they were as heavy as mountains. He could not budge them. Trembling for shame he said: "I came wanting the teaching, not the material treasures. Please teach me."

The sixth patriarch said: "When you do not think good and when you do not think not-good, what is your true self?"

At these words E-myo was illumined. Perspiration broke out all over his body. He cried and bowed, saying: "You have given me the secret words and meanings. Is there yet a deeper part of the teaching?"

The sixth patriarch replied: "What I have told you is no secret at all. When you realize your own true self the secret belongs to you."

E-myo said: "I was under the fifth patriarch many years but could not realize my true self until now. Through your teaching I find the source. A person drinks water and knows himself whether it is cold or warm. May I call you my teacher?"

The sixth patriarch replied: "We studied together under the fifth patriarch. Call him your teacher, but just treasure what you have attained."

Mumon's comment: The sixth patriarch certainly was kind in such an emergency. It was as if he removed the skin and seeds from the fruit and then, opening the pupil's mouth, let him eat.

> You cannot describe it, you cannot picture it,
> You cannot admire it, you cannot sense it.
> It is your true self, it has nowhere to hide.
> When the world is destroyed, it will not be destroyed.

WITHOUT WORDS, WITHOUT SILENCE

A monk asked Fuketsu: "Without speaking, without silence, how can you express the truth?"

Fuketsu observed: "I always remember springtime in southern China. The birds sing among innumerable kinds of fragrant flowers."

Mumon's comment: Fuketsu used to have lightning Zen. Whenever he had the opportunity, he flashed it. But this time he failed to do so and only borrowed from an old Chinese poem. Never mind Fuketsu's Zen. If you want to express the truth, throw out your words, throw out your silence, and tell me about your own Zen.

> Without revealing his own penetration,
> He offered another's words, not his to give.
> Had he chattered on and on,
> Even his listeners would have been embarrassed.

PREACHING FROM THE THIRD SEAT

In a dream Kyozan went to Maitreya's Pure Land. He recognized himself seated in the third seat in the abode of Maitreya. Someone announced: "Today the one who sits in the third seat will preach."

Kyozan arose and, hitting the gavel, said: "The truth of Mahayana teaching is transcendent, above words and thought. Do you understand?"

Mumon's comment: I want to ask you monks: Did he preach or did he not?

When he opens his mouth he is lost. When he seals his mouth he is lost. If he does not open it, if he does not seal it, he is 108,000 miles from truth.

> In the light of day,
> Yet in a dream he talks of a dream.
> A monster among monsters,
> He intended to deceive the whole crowd.

TWO MONKS ROLL UP THE SCREEN

Hogen of Seiryo monastery was about to lecture before dinner when he noticed that the bamboo screen lowered for meditation had not been rolled up. He pointed to it. Two monks arose from the audience and rolled it up.

Hogen, observing the physical moment, said: "The state of the first monk is good, not that of the other."

Mumon's comment: I want to ask you: Which of those two monks gained and which lost? If any of you has one eye, he will see the failure on the teacher's part. However, I am not discussing gain and loss.

> When the screen is rolled up the great sky opens,
> Yet the sky is not attuned to Zen.
> It is best to forget the great sky
> And to retire from every wind.

IT IS NOT MIND, IT IS NOT BUDDHA, IT IS NOT THINGS

A monk asked Nansen: "Is there a teaching no master ever preached before?"

Nansen said: "Yes, there is."

"What is it?" asked the monk.

Nansen replied: "It is not mind, it is not Buddha, it is not things."

Mumon's comment: Old Nansen gave away his treasure-words. He must have been greatly upset.

> Nansen was too kind and lost his treasure.
> Truly, words have no power.
> Even though the mountain becomes the sea,
> Words cannot open another's mind.

BLOW OUT THE CANDLE

Tokusan was studying Zen under Ryutan. One night he came to Ryutan and asked many questions. The teacher said: "The night is getting old. Why don't you retire?"

So Tokusan bowed and opened the screen to go out, observing: "It is very dark outside."

Ryutan offered Tokusan a lighted candle to find his way. Just as Tokusan received it, Ryutan blew it out. At that moment the mind of Tokusan was opened.

"What have you attained?" asked Ryutan. "From now on," said Tokusan, "I will not doubt the teacher's words."

The next day Ryutan told the monks at his lecture: "I see one monk among you. His teeth are like the sword tree, his mouth is like the blood bowl. If you hit him hard with a big stick, he will not even so much as look back at you. Someday he will mount the highest peak and carry my teaching there."

On that day, in front of the lecture hall, Tokusan burned to ashes his commentaries on the sutras. He said: "However abstruse the teachings are, in comparison with this enlightenment they are like a single hair to the great sky. However profound the complicated knowledge of the world, compared to this enlightenment it is like one drop of water to the great ocean." Then he left that monastery.

Mumon's comment: When Tokusan was in his own country he was not satisfied with Zen although he had heard about it. He thought: "Those Southern monks say they can teach Dharma outside of the sutras. They are all wrong. I must teach them." So he traveled south. He happened to stop near Ryutan's monastery for refreshments. An old woman who was there asked him: "What are you carrying so heavily?"

Tokusan replied: "This is a commentary I have made on the Diamond Sutra after many years of work."

The old woman said: "I read that sutra which says: 'The past mind cannot be held, the present mind cannot be held, the future mind cannot be held.' You wish some tea and refreshments. Which mind do you propose to use for them?"

Tokusan was as though dumb. Finally he asked the woman: "Do you know of any good teacher around here?"

The old woman referred him to Ryutan, not more than five miles away. So he went to Ryutan in all humility, quite different from when he had started his journey. Ryutan in turn was so kind he forgot his own dignity. It was like pouring muddy water over a drunken man to sober him. After all, it was an unnecessary comedy.

A hundred hearings cannot surpass one seeing,
But after you see the teacher, that one glance cannot surpass a hundred hearings.
His nose was very high
But he was blind after all.

NOT THE WIND, NOT THE FLAG

Two monks were arguing about a flag. One said: "The flag is moving."

The other said: "The wind is moving."

The sixth patriarch happened to be passing by. He told them: "Not the wind, not the flag; mind is moving."

Mumon's comment: The sixth patriarch said: "The wind is not moving, the flag is not moving. Mind is moving." What did he mean? If you understand this intimately, you will see the two monks there trying to buy iron and gaining gold. The sixth patriarch could not bear to see those two dull heads, so he made such a bargain.

> Wind, flag, mind moves,
> The same understanding.
> When the mouth opens
> All are wrong.

THIS MIND IS BUDDHA

Daibai asked Baso: "What is Buddha?"

Baso said: "This mind is Buddha."

Mumon's comment: If anyone wholly understands this, he is wearing Buddha's clothing, he is eating Buddha's food, he is speaking Buddha's words, he is behaving as Buddha, he is Buddha. This anecdote, however, has given many a pupil the sickness of formality. If one truly understands, he will wash out his mouth for three days after saying the word Buddha, and he will close his ears and flee after hearing "This mind is Buddha."

Under blue sky, in bright sunlight,
One need not search around.
Asking what Buddha is
Is like hiding loot in one's pocket and declaring oneself innocent.

JOSHU INVESTIGATES

A traveling monk asked an old woman the road to Taizan, a popular temple supposed to give wisdom to the one who worships there. The old woman said: "Go straight ahead." When the monk proceeded a few steps, she said to herself: "He also is a common church-goer."

Someone told this incident to Joshu, who said: "Wait until I investigate." The next day he went and asked the same question, and the old woman gave the same answer.

Joshu remarked: "I have investigated that old woman."

Mumon's comment: The old woman understood how war is planned, but she did not know how spies sneak in behind her tent. Old Joshu played the spy's work and turned the tables on her, but he was not an able general. Both had their faults. Now I want to ask you: What was the point of Joshu's investigating the old woman?

> When the question is common
> The answer is also common.
> When the question is sand in a bowl of boiled rice
> The answer is a stick in the soft mud.

A PHILOSOPHER ASKS BUDDHA

A philosopher asked Buddha: "Without words, without the wordless, will you tell me truth?"

The Buddha kept silence.

The philosopher bowed and thanked the Buddha, saying: "With your loving kindness I have cleared away my delusions and entered the true path."

After the philosopher had gone, Ananda asked the Buddha what he had attained.

The Buddha replied: "A good horse runs even at the shadow of the whip."

Mumon's comment: Ananda was the disciple of the Buddha. Even so, his opinion did not surpass that of outsiders. I want to ask you monks: How much difference is there between disciples and outsiders?

> To tread the sharp edge of a sword,
> To run on smooth-frozen ice,
> One needs no footsteps to follow.
> Walk over the cliffs with hands free.

THIS MIND IS NOT BUDDHA

A monk asked Baso: "What is Buddha?"

Baso said: "This mind is not Buddha."

Mumon's comment: If anyone understands this, he is a graduate of Zen.

If you meet a fencing-master on the road, you may give him your sword,
If you meet a poet, you may offer him your poem.
When you meet others, say only a part of what you intend.
Never give the whole thing at once.

LEARNING IS NOT THE PATH

Nansen said: "Mind is not Buddha. Learning is not the path."

Mumon's comment: Nansen was getting old and forgot to be ashamed. He spoke out with bad breath and exposed the scandal of his own home. However, there are few who appreciate his kindness.

> When the sky is clear the sun appears,
> When the earth is parched rain will fall.
> He opened his heart fully and spoke out,
> But it was useless to talk to pigs and fish.

TWO SOULS

"Seijo, the Chinese girl," observed Goso, "had two souls, one always sick at home and the other in the city, a married woman with two children. Which was the true soul?"

Mumon's comment: When one understands this, he will know it is possible to come out from one shell and enter another, as if one were stopping at a transient lodging house. But if he cannot understand, when his time comes and his four elements separate, he will be just like a crab dipped in boiling water, struggling with many hands and legs. In such a predicament he may say: "Mumon did not tell me where to go!" but it will be too late then.

> The moon above the clouds is the same moon,
> The mountains and rivers below are all different.
> Each is happy in its unity and variety.
> This is one, this is two.

MEETING A ZEN MASTER ON THE ROAD

Goso said: "When you meet a Zen master on the road you cannot talk to him, you cannot face him with silence. What are you going to do?"

Mumon's comment: In such a case, if you can answer him intimately, your realization will be beautiful, but if you cannot, you should look about without seeing anything.

> Meeting a Zen master on the road,
> Face him neither with words nor silence.
> Give him an uppercut
> And you will be called one who understands Zen.

A BUFFALO PASSES THROUGH THE ENCLOSURE

Goso said: "When a buffalo goes out of his enclosure to the edge of the abyss, his horns and his head and his hoofs all pass through, but why can't the tail also pass?"

Mumon's comment: If anyone can open one eye at this point and say a word of Zen, he is qualified to repay the four gratifications, and, not only that, he can save all sentient beings under him. But if he cannot say such a word of true Zen, he should turn back to his tail.

> If the buffalo runs, he will fall into the trench;
> If he returns, he will be butchered.
> That little tail
> Is a very strange thing.

AN OAK TREE IN THE GARDEN

A monk asked Joshu why Bodhidharma came to China.

Joshu said: "An oak tree in the garden."

Mumon's comment: If one sees Joshu's answer clearly, there is no Shakyamuni Buddha before him and no future Buddha after him.

Words cannot describe everything.
The heart's message cannot be delivered in words.
If one receives words literally, he will be lost,
If he tries to explain with words, he will not attain enlightenment in this life.

UMMON'S SIDETRACK

A Zen student told Ummon: "Brilliancy of Buddha illuminates the whole universe."

Before he finished the phrase Ummon asked: "You are reciting another's poem, are you not?"

"Yes," answered the student.

"You are sidetracked," said Ummon.

Afterwards another teacher, Shishin, asked his pupils: "At what point did that student go off the track?"

Mumon's comment: If anyone perceives Ummon's particular skillfulness, he will know at what point the student was off the track, and he will be a teacher of man and Devas. If not, he cannot even perceive himself.

> When a fish meets the fishhook
> If he is too greedy, he will be caught.
> When his mouth opens
> His life already is lost.

TIPPING OVER A WATER VASE

Hyakujo wished to send a monk to open a new monastery. He told his pupils that whoever answered a question most ably would be appointed. Placing a water vase on the ground, he asked: "Who can say what this is without calling its name?"

The chief monk said: "No one can call it a wooden shoe."

Isan, the cooking monk, tipped over the vase with his foot and went out.

Hyakujo smiled and said: "The chief monk loses." And Isan became the master of the new monastery.

Mumon's comment: Isan was brave enough, but he could not escape Hyakujo's trick. After all, he gave up a light job and took a heavy one. Why, can't you see, he took off his comfortable hat and placed himself in iron stocks.

> Giving up cooking utensils,
> Defeating the chatterbox,
> Though his teacher sets a barrier for him
> His feet will tip over everything, even the Buddha.

BODHIDHARMA PACIFIES THE MIND

Bodhidharma sits facing the wall. His future successor stands in the snow and presents his severed arm to Bodhidharma. He cries: "My mind is not pacified. Master, pacify my mind."

Bodhidharma says: "If you bring me that mind, I will pacify it for you."

The successor says: "When I search my mind I cannot hold it."

Bodhidharma says: "Then your mind is pacified already."

Mumon's comment: That broken-toothed old Hindu, Bodhidharma, came thousands of miles over the sea from India to China as if he had something wonderful. He is like raising waves without wind. After he remained years in China he had only one disciple and that one lost his arm and was deformed. Alas, ever since he has had brainless disciples.

> Why did Bodhidharma come to China?
> For years monks have discussed this.
> All the troubles that have followed since
> Came from that teacher and disciple.

THE GIRL COMES OUT FROM MEDITATION

In the time of Buddha Shakyamuni, Manjusri went to the assemblage of the Buddhas. When he arrived there, the conference was over and each Buddha had returned to his own Buddha-land. Only one girl was yet unmoved in deep meditation.

Manjusri asked Buddha Shakyamuni how it was possible for this girl to reach this state, one which even he could not attain. "Bring her out from Samadhi and ask her yourself," said the Buddha.

Manjusri walked around the girl three times and snapped his fingers. She still remained in meditation. So by his miracle power he transported her to a high heaven and tried his best to call her, but in vain.

Buddha Shakyamuni said: "Even a hundred thousand Manjusris could not disturb her, but below this place, past twelve hundred million countries, is a Bodhisattva, Mo-myo, seed of delusion. If he comes here, she will awaken."

No sooner had the Buddha spoken than that Bodhisattva sprang up from the earth and bowed and paid homage to the Buddha. Buddha directed him to arouse the girl. The Bodhisattva went in front of the girl and snapped his fingers, and in that instant the girl came out from her deep meditation.

Mumon's comment: Old Shakyamuni set a very poor stage. I want to ask you monks: If Manjusri, who is supposed to have been the teacher of seven Buddhas, could not bring this girl out of meditation, how then could a Bodhisattva who was a mere beginner?

If you understand this intimately, you yourself can enter the great meditation while you are living in the world of delusion.

> One could not awaken her, the other could.
> Neither are good actors.
> One wears the mask of god, one a devil's mask.
> Had both failed, the drama still would be a comedy.

SHUZAN'S SHORT STAFF

Shuzan held out his short staff and said: "If you call this a short staff, you oppose its reality. If you do not call it a short staff, you ignore the fact. Now what do you wish to call this?"

Mumon's comment: If you call this a short staff, you oppose its reality. If you do not call it a short staff, you ignore the fact. It cannot be expressed with words and it cannot be expressed without words. Now say quickly what it is.

> Holding out the short staff,
> He gave an order of life or death.
> Positive and negative interwoven,
> Even Buddhas and patriarchs cannot escape this attack.

BASHO'S STAFF

Basho said to his disciple: "When you have a staff, I will give it to you. If you have no staff, I will take it away from you."

Mumon's comment: When there is no bridge over the creek the staff will help me. When I return home on a moonless night the staff will accompany me. But if you call this a staff, you will enter hell like an arrow.

With this staff in my hand
I can measure the depths and shallows of the world.
The staff supports the heavens and makes firm the earth.
Everywhere it goes the true teaching will be spread.

WHO IS HE?

Hoen said: "The past and future Buddhas, both are his servants. Who is he?"

Mumon's comment: If you realize clearly who he is, it is as if you met your own father on a busy street. There is no need to ask anyone whether or not your recognition is true.

> Do not fight with another's bow and arrow.
> Do not ride another's horse.
> Do not discuss another's faults.
> Do not interfere with another's work.

PROCEED FROM THE TOP OF THE POLE

Sekiso asked: "How can you proceed on from the top of a hundred-foot pole?" Another Zen teacher said: "One who sits on the top of a hundred-foot pole has attained a certain height but still is not handling Zen freely. He should proceed on from there and appear with his whole body in the ten parts of the world."

Mumon's comment: One can continue his steps or turn his body freely about on the top of the pole. In either case he should be respected. I want to ask you monks, however: How will you proceed from the top of that pole? Look out!

> The man who lacks the third eye of insight
> Will cling to the measure of the hundred feet.
> Such a man will jump from there and kill himself,
> Like a blind man misleading other blind men.

THREE GATES OF TOSOTSU

Tosotsu built three barriers and made the monks pass through them. The first barrier is studying Zen. In studying Zen the aim is to see one's own true nature. Now where is your true nature?

Secondly, when one realizes his own true nature he will be free from birth and death. Now when you shut the light from your eyes and become a corpse, how can you free yourself?

Thirdly, if you free yourself from birth and death, you should know where you are. Now your body separates into the four elements. Where are you?

Mumon's comment: Whoever can pass these three barriers will be a master wherever he stands. Whatever happens about him he will turn into Zen.

Otherwise he will be living on poor food and not even enough of that to satisfy himself.

> An instant realization sees endless time.
> Endless time is as one moment.
> When one comprehends the endless moment
> He realizes the person who is seeing it.

ONE ROAD OF KEMBO

A Zen pupil asked Kembo: "All Buddhas of the ten parts of the universe enter the one road of Nirvana. Where does that road begin?"

Kembo, raising his walking stick and drawing the figure one in the air, said: "Here it is."

This pupil went to Ummon and asked the same question. Ummon, who happened to have a fan in his hand, said: "This fan will reach to the thirty-third heaven and hit the nose of the presiding deity there. It is like the Dragon Carp of the Eastern Sea tipping over the rain-cloud with his tail."

Mumon's comment: One teacher enters the deep sea and scratches the earth and raises dust. The other goes to the mountain top and raises waves that almost touch heaven. One holds, the other gives out. Each supports the profound teaching with a single hand. Kembo and Ummon are like two riders neither of whom can surpass the other. It is very difficult to find the perfect man. Frankly, neither of them know where the road starts.

> Before the first step is taken the goal is reached.
> Before the tongue is moved the speech is finished.
> More than brilliant intuition is needed
> To find the origin of the right road.

AMBAN'S ADDITION

Amban, a layman Zen student, said: "Mu-mon has just published forty-eight koans and called the book Gateless Gate. He criticizes the old patriarchs' words and actions. I think he is very mischievous. He is like an old doughnut seller trying to catch a passerby to force his doughnuts down his mouth. The customer can neither swallow nor spit out the doughnuts, and this causes suffering. Mu-mon has annoyed everyone enough, so I think I shall add one more as a bargain. I wonder if he himself can eat this bargain. If he can, and digest it well, it will be fine, but if not, we will have to put it back into the frying pan with his forty-eight also and cook them again. Mu-mon, you eat first, before someone else does:

"Buddha, according to a sutra, once said: 'Stop, stop. Do not speak. The ultimate truth is not even to think.'"

Amban's comment: Where did that so-called teaching come from? How is it that one could not even think it? Suppose someone spoke about it then what became of it? Buddha himself was a great chatterbox and in this sutra spoke contrarily. Because of this, persons like Mu-mon appear afterwards in China and make useless doughnuts, annoying people. What shall we do after all? I will show you.

Then Amban put his palms together, folded his hands, and said: "Stop, stop. Do not speak. The ultimate truth is not even to think. And now I will make a little circle on the sutra with my finger and add that five thousand other sutras and Vimalakirti's gateless gate all are here!"

If anyone tells you fire is light,
Pay no attention.
When two thieves meet they need no introduction:
They recognize each other without question.

www.ingramcontent.com/pod-product-compliance
Lightning Source LLC
Chambersburg PA
CBHW051606010526
44119CB00056B/807